The Fulfilling Ride

D1472237

The Fulfilling Ride

A Parent's Guide to Helping Athletes Have a
Successful Sport Experience

Greg Dale, Ph.D.

Cover photo by Jonathan Abels

Published by Excellence in Performance
11 Chimney Top Ct. Durham, NC 27705
www.excellenceinperformance.com
gdale@duke.edu
(919) 401-9640

If you are unable to order this book from your local
bookseller, you may order directly from the publisher.
gdale@duke.edu | (919) 401-9640

Library of Congress Control Number: 2005928794
ISBN 978-0-9755764-1-0
10 9 8 7 6 5 4 3 2 1
Printed on acid-free paper in the United States.

To my parents, Dolores and Shep, and all other parents who provide a healthy environment for their children to thrive in sport.

Table of Contents

Acknowledgments

There were many people who were instrumental in making this book possible. First I would like to thank my wife, Cammie, for her incredible support and willingness to help throughout the writing of this book. I couldn't have done it without her. Second, I would like to thank Mark Thomas for encouraging me to write the book and his never-ending support of the project. Third, I would like to thank Scott Yakola, Bart Lerner, Jeff Janssen, Sarah Naylor, Richard Ford, Shelley Wiechman and Chris Janelle, who were all willing to read drafts of the manuscript and provide valuable feedback.

Introduction

photo:New Jersey High School Athletic Association

If you are like most parents of athletes, you have asked yourself questions such as these at some point during your child's athletic career:

Should my child specialize in one sport to maximize her chances of success in today's world of athletics?

What are the odds of my child getting a college scholarship?

What should I expect from my child's coach?

What is the most effective way to approach my child's coach about a concern?

What should I do if I begin to feel that I "have no life" outside my child's sport?

Is it really that important for parents to model good sportsmanship when watching competitions?

How does it affect my child when I am "coaching" from the sidelines?

How can I help my child effectively handle the inevitable adversities that come with participating in sport?

Am I doing my part to ensure that my child is having a good overall sport experience?

Would my child say that I am a positive sport parent who keeps everything in perspective when it comes to sport?

These types of questions are not always easy to answer. However, this book addresses these and many similar questions, providing practical and proven strategies to help you maximize your role as a sport parent and create the best possible environment for your child to succeed.

The Culture of Youth and High School Sport in Our Society

Sport has played a significant role in my life for as long as I can remember. Growing up in rural Texas and Alaska, I have many fond memories of both organized and unorganized sport. I had the opportunity to play organized sport through various youth organizations, and these experiences were enjoyable in large part because of the perspectives my coaches and parents had on the whole experience. They worked hard to create an environment where having fun, following the rules of the game and viewing sport as a privilege were paramount.

The most fun I ever had in an organized youth sport was as a twelve-year-old on an American Legion Summer League baseball team in Alaska. Our team was comprised of a ragtag group of kids who loved to play baseball just for the sake of playing. It was a co-ed team because there weren't enough kids in either gender to make a full team. There were kids on the team who lived as far as fifty miles away—they didn't travel that far to be on the best team; they traveled that distance because it was the only team in the area. Some of our team members couldn't afford sneakers or baseball cleats, so they wore cowboy boots, work boots or any other type of shoes they had lying around the house. Our coach was the owner of the local trading post who didn't know a great deal about baseball. However, he loved what he was doing and made sure we had fun as well. Our field was on one corner of a small airstrip. We built our own backstop and were constantly picking up the rocks from the field. The rocks never went away, but it was our field and we took great pride in taking care of it.

We had *one* organized practice a week and played *one* game a week with other teams within a 100-mile radius. Even though we formally got together only a couple times a week, we spent countless hours on our makeshift baseball field playing games just because we loved being with each other and for the sheer joy of playing. There were no adults around. We picked the teams and made adjustments after a while if the teams weren't fair. It was our game.

It seems like children don't get much of an opportunity to play sport for the sake of pure enjoyment anymore. From the time our children are four years old, they are involved in organized sport, with adults making all of the rules and the decisions. Therefore, they never really learn to make those decisions on their own. I witnessed the results of this phenomenon first hand recently when I agreed to be the pitcher for both teams in a baseball game in my front yard that involved neighborhood children between the ages of six and ten. This group of children had a very difficult time deciding how to pick teams, how to determine who would bat first and who would play each position in the field. After observing these various scenarios with amazement for several minutes and wanting to merely get the game started, I reluctantly intervened and provided them with ideas on how to make those decisions. In essence, I had to organize the game for them.

The "over-organization" of sport on the part of adults is due partially to the fact that it is no longer safe to allow our kids to play unsupervised. However, a significant portion of this phenomenon is due to the elevated place that sport now holds in our society. It is a multi-billion-dollar business and there are huge rewards (i.e., college scholarship, money and fame) for the very few who participate at a high level. Unfortunately, the increased focus on sport has affected the environment in which children participate at the high school, middle school and youth levels.

As a professor of sport psychology and sport ethics, and in my role as a mental training coach at Duke University, I have a passion for trying to help create an environment in sport where young athletes can thrive rather than survive. As a consultant, I often have the opportunity to travel around the country speaking to coaches, athletes and the parents of athletes. No matter where I go, the issues seem to be the same. We have lost perspective on sport and its significance in our children's lives.

Changing the Culture of Youth and High School Sport in Our Society

The experience a child has in sport depends on all three parties—the athlete, the coach and the athlete's parent—doing their parts effectively. I certainly spend a large portion of my time attempting to educate coaches about the types of environments they create for the athletes they coach. The coaches and I discuss their definitions of success and where "winning at all costs" fits into those definitions. We discuss the importance of their credibility as leaders and what they can do to enhance rather than undermine it. They are challenged to critically examine many of the myths involving motivation and communication with athletes. I feel very confident about the impact these discussions with coaches are having on the culture within the coaching profession.

Along with coaches, we as parents play such an absolutely critical role in the experience our children will have in sport. This is true whether your child is a six-year-old soccer player in a youth program or a seventeen-year-old on a high school team. Thankfully, most parents realize the significance of this role and work diligently to create a healthy environment for their children in sport. Unfortunately, there are also a significant number of parents who create a less-than-ideal environment.

It is interesting to note that most parents really want what is best for their children. We enjoy watching them participate in sport. We are proud of them when they are successful. And whether we want to admit it or not, we all live vicariously through our children at some level. The problem is that some parents take it too far and move from being supportive to being pushy, often without even realizing it.

I am now a parent of children who participate in sport and as a result, this book is a labor of love for me. My goal is to help you (and myself) as sport parents keep everything in perspective. I hope I am able to reinforce some of your actions as a parent and make you feel good about the role you play in your child's sport experience. I also hope that I might be able to encourage you to critically examine your behavior and determine if there is anything you might do differently to create a more positive environment for your athlete.

Most parents have a sense of what is right and wrong, and this book is not intended to be a lesson on morality. Rather, its intent is to provide a model of parental behavior that might allow children to have a successful sport experience. This model is based on my experiences working with athletes, coaches, athletic administrators and parents over the past fifteen years. After reading this book you should have more insight into the impact you have as a parent and into the importance of making sure that every decision you make and every action you take are in the best interest of your child's development for a lifetime.

Whether your child is on a youth team or is a varsity athlete in high school, you will find this book applicable to you. Whenever possible, age-appropriate examples are provided to highlight material that is more appropriate for one age group over another. I encourage you to read the book with an open mind. Make a conscious effort to avoid thoughts such as, "This doesn't really apply to me," "I hope so-and-so's dad reads this book because he really needs to hear the message," or "This book was written for parents like ..." Instead, think about how each of the points applies to *you*, your role in your child's sport experience and whether or not you need to change your outlook or behaviors. Your child will certainly be glad you did.

Layout of the Book

The book is divided into five sections in which you will be provided food for thought in areas in which you have direct influence upon your child's sport experience. The first section is designed to help you and your child assess your current effectiveness as a sport parent. The second section provides ideas to help you create the best possible environment for your child in sport. Here, you will be challenged to examine the general attitude you create towards the overall sport experience. The third section will challenge you to examine your basic role as a sport parent, as well as your interactions with other parents and their children at sporting events. The fourth section will encourage you to examine your interactions with those who coach your child and determine whether or not you are doing your part to make sure you and the coach are working toward the same goals. The fifth section helps you examine how you interact with your child before, during and after competition.

The Use of "He" and "She"

Every attempt has been made to represent both male and female gender groups by using "he" and "she" throughout the book. For the sake of sentence flow, "he/she" is used on a very limited basis. However, it is important to note that "he" and "she" are interchangeable in that each of the principles discussed in the book relates to both genders.

Assessing Your Effectiveness as a Sport Parent

photo by Phil Travis

"I definitely love sports, and winning is huge for me. But it isn't everything to me. I like being part of a team and knowing that I contribute to the team's success is a big part of why I play."

—Fourteen-year-old Soccer Player

- *Have you ever wondered why your child participates in sport?*
- *What is it that draws us to sport when we are young?*
- *Why do children stop playing a particular sport?*
- *Are you doing everything you can to ensure that your child is enjoying his sport experience?*
- *How do you determine your success as a sport parent?*
- *Is your child proud of how you play the role of a sport parent?*

I t is interesting to note that when I ask children why they participate in sport, they say it is fun, they enjoy being with their friends, they enjoy competition, they like doing something they are good at, and they hope to improve their skills. Winning is certainly one of the reasons they give because they do enjoy winning. However, it isn't everything to them. This should be a sign that we as parents need to place winning in its proper place when we think about the benefits of participating in sport.

While it is important for parents to know why children participate in sport, it is even more important to determine why children *stop* participating in sport. As they grow older, children lose interest in sport for various reasons. Some simply find other areas of their lives that interest them more. There are also more negative reasons for stopping, such as they aren't having as much fun anymore, they feel too much pressure to perform well or win and their coaches aren't very effective teachers of the sport.

As parents, we clearly have a significant influence over whether our kids have fun in sport and whether they feel too much pressure to win or play well. However, we can choose to take a more positive role in their sport experience. We can allow and encourage them to have fun. We can avoid putting excess pressure on them. And, we can de-emphasize winning, and focus more on the lessons that sport can teach our children about being successful in life.

You will be provided with strategies to accomplish all of these throughout the remainder of this book. However, I encourage you to begin thinking now about how you might improve in these areas. One way to begin this process is for you and your child to utilize the age-appropriate assessments provided for you in the next few pages. If conducted objectively, these assessments shed valuable light on your current role as a sport parent. There is a self-assessment in which you will have the opportunity to honestly reflect on how you feel you rate as an effective sport parent. A second assessment is designed to allow your child to rate you on her perception of your effectiveness as a sport parent. You will most likely need to explain some of the terminology if you have a younger child filling out an assessment on you. However, your child should be allowed to assess you without your influence if at all possible.

Once you have both responded to the assessments, it will be important to compare the results. In comparing the responses, you should determine the overall results. Be prepared for any scenario (i.e., Does your child rate you higher than you rate yourself? Is it the other way around?) and be willing to discuss the results with your child. If your child gives you a lower overall rating than you gave yourself, it is critical that you determine the reasons. It is also important to examine each statement individually and note your child's rating. For example, your child might have given you an overall high rating, but a low rating on "My parent does not coach me or any of my teammates from the sidelines." Find out why your child gave you that lower rating and make a commitment to him that you will work very hard to change in that area if it is having a negative effect on his sport experience.

By taking the time to honestly and objectively reflect on your role as a sport parent and by being willing to listen to the feedback your child gives you, you are setting the tone for your child to have a successful sport experience. Make sure you revisit these assessments periodically throughout the year and your child's sport career. If you do so, you will have a much better chance of being a successful sport parent.

Parent Self-Assessment
for Parents of Athletes Ages 7-13

Using a scale from one to five, rate yourself on your effectiveness as a sport parent.

1	2	3	4	5
Strongly Disagree	**Disagree**	**Undecided**	**Agree**	**Strongly Agree**

__ *I model good sportsmanship at all competitions in the way I interact with parents, athletes, coaches, and officials.*

__ *I conduct myself in a manner such that my family and friends enjoy sitting next to me during competitions.*

__ *I do not put too much pressure on my child to win or perform exceptionally well.*

__ *I do not compare my child to other children.*

__ *I do not criticize my child's coach in front of my child.*

__ *I do not provide technical or strategic instructions to my child or other athletes during competition.*

__ *I allow and encourage my child to participate in multiple sports rather than specializing in one sport all year long.*

__ *I provide total and unconditional love and support for my child, regardless of how he or she performs.*

__ *I do not expect any type of monetary return (i.e., college scholarship, professional contract) on the time and money I spend on my child's sport.*

__ *I conduct myself in a manner that makes my child proud to have me in attendance.*

___ Total

Score
45-50 Excellent: You are a model sport parent.
40-44 Very Good: Communicate with your child to maintain your current perspective.
30-39 Cause for Concern: Be willing to listen and make changes to regain a proper perspective.
1-29 Out of Control: You have lost perspective. You could be in danger of ruining your child's sport experience.

Athlete Assessment of a Parent
for Athletes Ages 7-13

Using a scale from one to five, rate your parent on his or her effectiveness as a sport parent.

1	2	3	4	5
Strongly Disagree	Disagree	Undecided	Agree	Strongly Agree

___ *My parent is a good sport at all my games because he or she does not yell at referees, coaches, or players.*

___ *Everyone else in my family enjoys sitting next to my parent at my games.*

___ *My parent does not put too much pressure on me to win.*

___ *My parent does not compare me to other kids.*

___ *My parent does not talk bad about my coach in front of me.*

___ *My parent does not coach me or any of my teammates from the sidelines while we are playing.*

___ *My parent encourages me to play more than one sport, instead of focusing on just one all year long.*

___ *My parent treats me the same way whether I play well or not.*

___ *My parent does not talk a lot about me getting a college scholarship or playing professionally some day.*

___ *I am proud to have my parent at my games.*

___ **Total**

Score

45-50 Excellent: You are a model sport parent.

40-44 Very Good: Communicate with your child to maintain your current perspective.

30-39 Cause for Concern: Be willing to listen and make changes to regain a proper perspective.

1-29 Out of Control: Your child feels you have lost perspective. You could be in danger of ruining your child's sport experience.

Parent Self-Assessment
for Parents of Athletes Ages 14-18

Using a scale from one to five, rate yourself on your effectiveness as a sport parent.

1	2	3	4	5
Strongly Disagree	**Disagree**	**Undecided**	**Agree**	**Strongly Agree**

___ *I model good sportsmanship at all competitions in the way I interact with other parents, athletes, coaches and officials.*

___ *I conduct myself in a manner such that my family and friends enjoy sitting next to me during competitions.*

___ *I do not put too much pressure on my child to win or perform exceptionally well.*

___ *I allow and encourage my child to talk to the coach if he or she has an issue with the coach before intervening myself.*

___ *I do not criticize my child's coach in front of my child.*

___ *I do not give technical or strategic instructions to my child or other athletes during competition.*

___ *I plan to allow and encourage my child to participate in multiple sports, rather than specializing in one sport, until he or she has finished high school.*

___ *I provide total and unconditional love and support for my child regardless of how he or she performs.*

___ *I do not expect any type of monetary return (i.e., college scholarship, professional contract) on the time and money I spend on my child's sport.*

___ *I conduct myself in a manner that makes my child proud to have me in attendance.*

___ **Total**

Score

45-50 **Excellent:** You are a model sport parent.

40-44 **Very Good:** Communicate with your child to maintain your current perspective.

30-39 **Cause for Concern:** Be willing to listen and make changes to regain a proper perspective.

1-29 **Out of Control:** You have lost perspective. You could be in danger of ruining your child's sport experience.

Athlete Assessment of a Parent
for Athletes Ages 14-18

Using a scale from one to five, rate your parent on his or her effectiveness as a sport parent.

1 **Strongly** **Disagree**	**2** **Disagree**	**3** **Undecided**	**4** **Agree**	**5** **Strongly** **Agree**

_ *My parent demonstrates good sportsmanship at all competitions in the way he/she interacts with other parents, athletes, coaches, and officials.*

_ *My parent acts in a way such that everyone else in my family enjoys sitting next to him or her during competitions.*

_ *My parent does not put too much pressure on me to win or perform exceptionally well.*

_ *My parent allows and encourages me to talk to the coach if I have an issue with the coach before he or she intervenes.*

_ *My parent does not criticize my coach in front of me.*

_ *My parent does not coach me or any of my teammates from the sidelines while we are competing.*

_ *My parent will allow and encourage me to participate in multiple sports, instead of specializing in one sport, all the way through high school.*

_ *My parent provides total and unconditional love and support for me regardless of how I perform.*

_ *My parent does not expect any type of monetary return (i.e., college scholarship, professional contract) on the time and money he or she spends on my sport.*

_ *I am proud to have my parent attend my competitions.*

___ **Total**

Score
45-50 Excellent: You are a model sport parent.
40-44 Very Good: Communicate with your child to maintain your current perspective.
30-39 Cause for Concern: Be willing to listen and make changes to regain a proper perspective.
1-29 Out of Control: Your child feels you have lost perspective. You could be in danger of ruining your child's sport experience.

Key Points to Remember

- *Children of all ages participate in sport primarily because it is fun.*
- *As a sport parent, you can create a situation where your child enjoys participating in sport.*
- *Be willing to assess your effectiveness as a sport parent.*
- *Allow your child to provide you with feedback regarding his or her perception of your effectiveness.*
- *Be willing to make any necessary changes to ensure you are creating an environment where your child can flourish.*

Your Athlete and the Overall Sport Environment

photo by Jonathan Abels

"It is funny how parents tell us to be good sports and do things the right way in sport, but I see so many parents who are out of control and don't have a clue about the message they send when they act that way."

—*Eighteen-Year-Old Swimmer*

- *Do you know the lessons you want your child to learn from participating in sport?*
- *Do you model the lessons you want your child to learn in sport?*
- *Do you and your child view participation in sport as a privilege or a right?*
- *Is your child specializing in one sport year-round?*
- *Do you emphasize and reward effort and attitude over results?*

Two questions I always like to ask parents of athletes are, "What are the lessons you hope your child learns from participating in sport?" and "What do you hope your child gains from a sport experience?" Regardless of the age of their children, parents will say they want them to learn lessons like sportsmanship, teamwork, self-discipline, overcoming adversity, respect for authority and commitment, to name a few. At that point, I begin to encourage parents to remember that they have a responsibility to model the lessons they want athletes to learn. Participation in sport does provide exceptional opportunities to learn these great life lessons. Unfortunately, young athletes are not going to learn these lessons from what they observe on television or in the collegiate or professional models of sport. Acts of unsportsmanlike conduct and cheating such as trash-talking, taunting, fighting and taking steroids are sensationalized in the media. And our children tend to pattern their behavior after their idols and what they see on television.

As a sport parent, you should teach your child that sportsmanship and respect for the game and the opponent are important ways to measure one's success. Take it upon yourself to teach these lessons by modeling them yourself. The following are a few areas you can focus on to ensure that your child learns valuable lessons from participating in sport.

Participating in Sport Is a Privilege

It seems that many parents have lost this idea somewhere along the way. Some parents have a difficult time when their child moves from youth league teams, where all athletes get to participate, to middle and high school teams where playing time is at the coach's discretion. However, the most likely reason most parents have difficulty with this is because they invest so much more time and money in sport today than in the past.

It is very important to instill in young athletes, from the very beginning, that participating in sport is a privilege that should never be taken for granted. It isn't something that is their right just because their parents pay money or invest an inordinate amount of time in it. I know of two college coaches who have made a decision to avoid recruiting athletes from one particular metropolitan area because too many of the athletes and their parents view participation in their sport, as well as a college scholarship, as their right rather than a privilege. This particular city is widely known as the "hotbed" of talent for this particular sport; children begin playing at a very early age and their parents spend a great deal of time and money to ensure they are competitive with the other children in the area. These coaches have long recruited athletes from this area, but find that they have much more difficulty dealing with the athletes and the parents who often make unreasonable demands, and ultimately make life difficult for the coach if those demands are not met.

Sportsmanship

Jim Thompson, a former professor at Stanford University, has initiated a very influential youth sports organization called the

Positive Coaching Alliance. The mission of this organization is to "transform sports so sports can transform youth." The Alliance is attempting to change the culture of winning at all cost that has trickled down to the youth sport level. Their focus is on educating coaches, athletes and parents about the importance of emphasizing the life lessons that can be learned from sport and honoring the game. Honoring the game means that all involved demonstrate respect for each other and avoid doing anything that takes away from the integrity of the sport. Certainly a significant aspect of honoring the game is sportsmanship. Is sportsmanship a lesson you want your child to learn while participating in sport? Does your child have a true respect for her sport and her opponents? Most importantly, are you modeling sportsmanship and respect for those involved in the sport in the way that you conduct yourself during competitions?

It can be amazing how people act so differently at a sporting event than they do anywhere else in their daily lives. It is almost as if being spectators at a sporting event gives some people license to say just about anything they want to officials, coaches and athletes. Part of this is due to the mob mentality in that people are much more likely to say and do things they wouldn't do otherwise when they will not be singled out from the group. Part of it is the culture of sport. Booing and degrading those participating in a competition has long been seen as part of the game. Officials seem to receive the brunt of most of the degrading comments from those in the stands. If you are a parent who participates in these actions, remember that officials are human and will make calls that you disagree with. However, if you boo them or scream obscenities at them, you are demonstrating poor sportsmanship and a lack of respect for authority. Another point to consider in this situation is to imagine what it would be like if several hundred people came to your place of employment and watched you do your job. Imagine that while observing you, people in the crowd began to yell at you and make derogatory remarks every time they felt you made a mistake. How might that affect your ability to concentrate or do your job effectively?

You certainly don't have to agree with officials, but it is imperative that you model a respectful way to handle your frustrations. Remember, your child is watching you and if you can show restraint in these situations, your child might be more likely to do so when she is in similar situations.

This was reinforced for me when I recently took my ten-year-old daughter, Abbey, to a Duke University Men's Basketball game. She was cheering for the Blue Devils and having a great time. About midway through the first half, she noticed a boy and his father booing and making derogatory remarks when officials made calls that were against Duke. My daughter then began to boo but she really didn't know why she was booing. She was clearly modeling the behavior that was being demonstrated to her.

Another aspect of honoring the game and sportsmanship is to encourage athletes to view their opponents as worthy foes rather than "the enemy." You might think this mentality softens an athlete, but I would argue that viewing the opponent in this manner teaches our children that they can have a healthy respect for their opponents and still be very competitive. If they are taught to hate their opponents, they will likely be more tolerant of behavior that takes away from the integrity of the sport and do whatever it takes to beat them.

The mentality of doing whatever it takes to win is a final aspect of honoring the game I would like for you to consider. Simply put, young athletes and their parents are cheating more than ever to ensure they have a better chance to win. A physician giving his fourteen-year-old son steroids so he can hit the baseball further, a father encouraging his high school son to use a lubricant on his football jersey to keep his opponents from tackling him, a mother telling her ten-year-old daughter that it is okay to cheat her opponent on line calls in tennis, and parents who lie on their residency papers so their child can play on a better team are all sending a very clear message: *Winning* is valued more than anything else. If you encourage or help your child cheat in any manner to gain an advantage over an opponent, you are making a mockery of the concept of pure competition. In the case of allowing or encouraging your child to take steroids or other performance-enhancing drugs, you are also seriously jeopardizing his health in the future.

In addition, it is important to remember that young children are very impressionable. If parents teach them to cheat in sport when they are learning the difference between right and wrong, they might be more likely to think it is okay to cheat in other aspects of life.

Many parents justify teaching or encouraging their children to cheat by saying that everyone else is doing it and they have to do it to be competitive. Russell Gough, in his book *Character Is Everything: Promoting Ethical Excellence in Sports,* says that the reason we cheat is not because everyone else is cheating; rather, it is ultimately because of something we want. For example, we cheat because we want to win, to succeed, to be famous. If you teach your child to cheat in any manner, you are making a strong statement that you want to win at any cost. In the end, the cost of this attitude could be your honor and integrity. Worse yet, it could mean your child's honor and integrity will be sacrificed. I encourage you to resist the temptation of falling into this mind-set. Teach your child that it is a hollow victory if you have to cheat to win. Teach him that even though others around him may be "doing whatever it takes to win," he will gain more satisfaction in the long run knowing he competed the way a true athlete competes.

Teamwork

Teamwork is certainly a lesson athletes will take with them for the rest of their lives. Parents often undermine the importance of teamwork without even realizing it. One way this occurs is when children are given monetary rewards for individual accomplishments. For example, if you pay your daughter money when she scores goals in soccer or your son when he scores baskets in basketball, you are sending the message that individual statistics are more important than the team. In this type of situation, the athlete will often take ill-advised shots, instead of passing the ball to a more open teammate because she wants to earn money for herself.

In addition to undermining the team-first concept, the practice of paying athletes for individual accomplishments can also diminish the intrinsic motivation to participate. In essence, they will begin to move from playing the sport because they enjoy it to playing the sport to receive monetary compensation. They are robbed of the joy of playing just to play.

Emphasize Effort and Attitude

Jeff Janssen, a friend and colleague, tells an inspirational story of an athlete in his book *Championship Team Building*. The athlete was Josh Pastner, a member of the 1997 Arizona Wildcats Basketball team that won a national championship. Josh wasn't one of the stars on the team. In fact, he only played in situations where the outcome of the game was clear. At the end of this championship season, Josh was voted the team's most valuable player by his teammates. Josh clearly didn't receive this award because of his superior talent. He was recognized for the superior attitude and effort that he brought to practice every day. He pushed his teammates to improve and worked hard in everything he did, despite the fact that he rarely ever played.

The moral of this story is that there is no correlation between an athlete's talent level and his attitude and effort. He can be the most talented athlete on the team or the least talented athlete on the team. It really doesn't matter. Either way, he can choose to have a positive attitude and work hard each and every day.

Over the last fifteen years consulting with athletes at all levels, I have found that athletes on a team are not remembered by their teammates primarily for the number of points or goals they scored or how many great games they played. They are remembered primarily for their attitude, effort and the type of teammate they are on a daily basis.

Like Josh, your child is not in control of how many points she scores or whether she is in the starting lineup. She is, however, in control of her attitude and effort and whether or not she is viewed as a good teammate. As a parent you can help your child focus more on her attitude and effort by encouraging her to always think about what is best for the team rather than what is in her personal best interest. Josh wasn't the star player on his team, but he didn't gripe and complain about not getting more playing time or become a negative influence on his teammates. Rather, he embraced his role and performed that role to the best of his ability to help his team succeed.

One way that I challenge athletes regarding their team-first attitude is to ask them to reflect on their actions during a competition when they aren't playing the role they want. A classic example is of the athlete who feels he should be playing, but is on the sidelines with others who are not playing. Without question, this can be a very challenging situation for an athlete who is competitive and wants to play. That said, the athlete has a choice in this situation: He can become withdrawn and refuse to cheer for his teammates, or he can choose to have a great attitude, embrace his role at that moment and encourage his teammates to the best of his ability.

Another opportunity to demonstrate a team-first attitude is after a competition is over and an athlete didn't get to play the role he wanted to play in that competition. If he withdraws from his teammates and doesn't join in the celebration of a hard-fought victory, he is sending a very strong message that he feels he is more important than the team. Athletes don't have to like that they didn't get to play the role they wanted, but they should demonstrate an attitude that they are happy for the team and join in the celebration.

Some parents actually undermine a good attitude because of their inability to remove their own egos from the situation. As mentioned earlier, we all want our children to do well and we live vicariously through them at some level. Just like a competitive athlete having a difficult time with a diminished role, you might very well struggle if your child is not playing the role you feel he deserves. However, if you are a parent who focuses more on your child's playing time and whether she starts or plays a lot rather than her attitude and effort, you are not doing your part to teach the importance of the team-first attitude. Teach your child to embrace her role and reinforce the importance of always focusing on what she is in control of—her attitude, effort, and role on the team. She will likely have a much better sport experience if you do.

Responsibility and Commitment

Responsibility and commitment are obviously lessons parents want their children to learn, and sport can be a great vehicle for teaching those lessons. One very important way you can model both of these is to make sure you get your child to practices and games on time. It is important for athletes at a very early age to realize that if they are going to make the commitment to a sport and a team, they are responsible and accountable. You send the wrong message if you don't also do your best to make sure your child is consistently on time to practices and competitions.

Children can also take some responsibility by making sure they have their sport equipment ready for practice each day.

A second aspect of responsibility and commitment is for athletes to stay with a sport or on a team for the duration of a season once it starts. The choice whether or not to begin a season should always be up to the child, but she has to learn that she must stick with it through the entire season. She can then re-evaluate whether or not she wants to continue once the season is finished. By taking this approach, she will definitely learn the value of finishing something she starts, regardless of how difficult it might be.

An issue that has become a major conflict for many athletes is juggling their time and commitments between club and school teams that compete during the same season. The potential negative effects of an athlete participating in multiple sports in one season are discussed in further detail later in this section of the book (see "Avoid Specializing in One Sport at a Young Age," page 29). Because school teams typically have one competitive season and club teams often have multiple seasons in a year, it seems important for athletes to commit to the school team during that one season. For example, if your child has club team practice or a tournament out of town that conflicts with a school team's schedule, your child should adhere to his commitment to the school team. It doesn't seem fair to the athletes and coaches from the school team if they cannot depend on your child to always be there during the short time they have together as a team. It will not always be easy for your child to choose, but once again this situation provides a very important life lesson about choices and commitment.

Overcoming Adversity

Many athletes must face adversity at some point during their athletic careers, and two common trials are being cut from a team and injuries. You can help your child learn from both of these situations by encouraging her to choose to view them as challenges she can overcome rather than negative situations that aren't fair. For the most part, both of these situations are out of your child's control, and as with all aspects of life, your child's success will not necessarily depend on what happens to her. Rather, it will depend largely on how she responds to what happens to her.

Being cut from a team does not have to be a completely devastating experience for your child. Initially, it will be important to empathize with your child and let him know your love and support are not dependent on athletic prowess in any way. However, it is equally important for you to encourage your child to respond to the situation as a challenge and determine what he needs to do to improve. If your child is younger, you can ask the coach what he needs to work on to improve his chances of making the team in the future. If your child is in middle school or high school, he should ask the coach himself (see "Approaching Your Child's Coach" on page 56 for more information on age-appropriateness when communicating with the coach). Once your child has been given specific skills to improve, help him establish a plan for working on those skills with the idea that you might be an integral part of that process.

A great example of an athlete responding in a positive manner to being cut involved a seventh-grade boy. After being cut from his team, the boy worked diligently to improve his areas of weakness that the coach pointed out. However, he also asked the coach if he could still come to practices and observe the team when they were practicing. During these practices, he took notes and became a much better student of the game. This particular boy made the team that next season and went on to have a very successful high school basketball career, culminating with him being named captain of the team his senior year. He clearly approached this situation as a challenge and ultimately rose above it.

Sustaining a serious injury causes a great deal of anguish and frustration for many athletes. In fact, athletes dealing with serious injuries often go through the same five-stage grief process we associate with the death of a loved one (Hardy & Crace, 1990). The familiar stages of Denial, Anger, Bargaining, Depression, and Acceptance/Reorganization do not occur in any set order and some athletes never experience all of the emotions. Those experiencing this process typically deny that the injury is in fact serious. They become angry and feel it is unfair that the injury happened to them. They bargain with doctors, trainers and others involved in the rehabilitation process to determine if they can return to their sport sooner. At some point, most athletes accept the injury and begin to establish a plan for rehabilitation. Other reactions to injury might include identity loss, fear, anxiety and lack of confidence (Petipas & Danish, 1995). As a parent, you can help your child through these various emotions by providing unconditional love and support and encouraging her to view the injury as a challenge without putting too much pressure on her to move to the acceptance and reorganization stages.

By helping your child respond to these and other adverse situations in a positive manner, you will help prepare her for life after sport. She will certainly face setbacks throughout life, and having dealt with potentially devastating adversity in sport, she will have a much better chance of responding in an appropriate manner when those setbacks occur.

Obviously there are numerous lessons children can learn from sport. These are just a few that I often hear parents mention. Take the time to identify the four or five lessons you feel are most important for your child to learn and make it your personal goal to focus on those lessons.

Avoid Specializing in One Sport at a Young Age

One of the truly great myths that is pervasive in sports today is that you have to specialize in a sport early and compete in that sport year-round in order to be successful. There are numerous reasons for this mentality and several are mentioned throughout this book (e.g., pressure to be competitive, drive to earn a college scholarship). Another source of this mentality comes from coaches. Some coaches pressure athletes into playing one sport year-round because they want the teams they coach to win. Some club team coaches attempt to persuade parents and athletes to specialize in the sport they coach because it is their source of income. While both of these examples represent a relatively small percentage of school and club coaches, the numbers seem to increase each year. With this in mind, make an attempt to determine the coach's motives when he or she is trying to convince your child to focus on one sport throughout the year.

A question I often get from parents around the country is, "When is it okay for my child to specialize in one sport?" My answer to them is that it almost never is. That is, at least until they are out of high school. There are numerous examples of elite athletes competing at the highest levels who competed in multiple sports all the way through high school. I recently had a panel of twelve student athletes from Duke speak to a group of coaches at a coaches' academy we conducted. These athletes represented sports such as men's and women's soccer, basketball, lacrosse, track and field, golf, football, wrestling, and rowing. During the Q and A portion of the panel discussion, one of the coaches in the audience asked the student athletes how many of them competed in only one sport in high school. Interestingly enough, all twelve of them competed in more than one sport throughout their high school careers. Similarly in my work as a mental training coach with college and professional athletes, I find that the overwhelming majority of them participated in more than one sport throughout their high school careers.

An athlete doesn't have to focus on one sport to be successful. There are certainly exceptions to this rule. With the support (and often encouragement) of their parents, some athletes choose to focus on one sport year-round from a very early age and grow up to be elite athletes. However, those athletes are truly *the exceptions* to the rule and shouldn't be held as the model to emulate.

There are many benefits that come from your child participating in more than one sport. For example, someone who plays soccer in the fall season will benefit greatly from playing basketball in the winter and softball in the spring. Mike Huff, Coordinator of Sports Performance at the Michael W. Krzyzewski Human Performance Lab at Duke University, says playing multiple sports exposes young athletes to a variety of movement skills that are necessary for athletic development. He indicates there are many baseball players who focus exclusively on baseball who can pitch or hit well, but have never really learned how to run properly. Or he has seen tennis players who can move well in a limited area on the tennis court and hit the ball well, but they have a difficult time getting to wider shots very quickly because they haven't developed their speed and quickness.

According to Mike, a second factor to consider when limiting a child's repertoire of skills by specializing in only one sport is that regardless of how many hours and how much money is spent on developing his talent in one sport, he might or might not be talented enough to earn a college scholarship or get drafted. However, there is a possibility the child could be an outstanding basketball player or track athlete if only given the chance to try. The problem is that he will never know if he is never exposed to those sports.

A third factor that Mike feels is critical to consider when determining whether children should participate in one sport is the increased likelihood of overuse injuries and burnout when they do. He regularly sees young athletes with tears of ligaments and tendons in the shoulder and elbow, cracked kneecaps, ankle injuries and growth plate problems because they don't take a break from their one sport. Orthopedic surgeons and doctors in pediatric sports medicine are also witnessing an alarming increase in overuse injuries in young athletes. Bill Pennington (2005) recently wrote in a New York *Times* article, "It is as if they have happened upon a new childhood disease, and the cause is the overaggressive culture of organized youth sports." Dr. Lyle Micheli, the director of sports medicine at Boston Children's Hospital, says that only 10 percent of the patients he treated 25 years ago suffered from overuse injuries. However, he indicates that 70 percent of his cases are now due to overuse injuries. Finally, Dr. James Andrews, a well-respected sports orthopedist in Birmingham, Alabama, cannot believe the types of injuries he is repeatedly seeing with thirteen- and fourteen-year-old children. The "wear and tear" he sees on the bodies of these children is hard to believe because those conditions have traditionally been reserved for much older athletes. Dr. Andrews is very clear in his views on how to alleviate this epidemic. He feels athletes must stop playing one sport year round, and they should "take three months off" from that sport before participating in it again. Because he works extensively with young baseball and softball players, he feels the use of radar guns in those sports should be banned to decrease the likelihood of pitchers overthrowing and potentially ruining their arms (Pennington, 2005).

The advice from all of the experts who have witnessed the increase in overuse injuries is to expose children to many activities and allow for adequate rest so they will become more well-rounded athletes. They will also have an opportunity to rest specific muscle groups and bones and will be much less likely to experience burnout and overuse injuries when they change sports with the changing seasons. Even taking some time away from all sports is a good idea.

Whatever you and your child decide in all of this, it is important to weigh the pros and cons of participating in one sport year-round. Educate your child about the benefits of participating in multiple sports and the two of you make an educated decision.

Key Points to Remember

- *Your child's participation in sport should be viewed as a privilege rather than a right regardless of the time and money you might spend on that experience.*

- *Your child can learn valuable life lessons such as sportsmanship, teamwork, responsibility and commitment, and overcoming adversity by participating in sport.*

- *It is important to model the lessons you want your child to learn in sport.*

- *Help your child realize the importance of focusing on effort and attitude.*

- *Resist buying into the myth that your child must participate in one sport year-round to be successful.*

Your Role as a Sport Parent and Your Interactions with Other Parents

photo by Phil Travis

"I am amazed, sometimes even shocked, at what I hear some parents say about children from their son or daughter's own team. They don't really care who might be listening or whose feelings they might hurt with the things they say."

—Parent of a Little League Baseball Player

- *Are you respectful of other parents and their children at sporting events?*
- *Are you a parent who feels you must attend many or all of your child's practice sessions?*
- *Do you ever feel you "have no life" outside your child's sport?*
- *Do you view the time and money you spend on your child's sport as an investment for which you expect a return?*
- *Do you know the basic rules of your child's sport?*
- *Are you under-involved in your child's sport?*

Policing Your Own Behavior

Proper parental behavior at competitions begins with you. What I mean by that is that each of us must be responsible for our own behavior as spectators and fans. While this section provides suggestions on how to effectively deal with other parents, I encourage you to first reflect on your own behavior and whether or not you are contributing to a positive environment on the sidelines. By critically examining whether you are respectful of others, whether you are a good representative of your child's team, and whether your loved ones enjoy sitting next to you during competitions, you will be well on your way to doing your part as a positive sport parent.

Be Respectful of Other Parents and Their Children

One of the main reasons parents get into arguments and sometimes fight with each other in the stands is because some parents do not respect other parents and their children. I have personally heard comments that are very disrespectful during high school competitions. Two such examples include, "Why is coach putting that kid in the game? He can't play!" or "She always seems to choke when the pressure is on at the end of the game. Coach better not put her in again or we will lose." As a fan in the stands, always be aware that when you make negative comments about an athlete, his parents are very likely sitting within range to hear you. Think about how it might make you feel if you heard someone saying something negative about your son or daughter. It is one thing to have these thoughts, but you must keep the negative comments to yourself or face the possibility of being confronted by an angry parent defending his or her child.

Another situation that often causes conflict among parents in the stands is when someone applauds a mistake made by an athlete on the opposing team. Once again, keep in mind how it would make you feel if someone were applauding when your child made a mistake. Not only will restraint in this situation help alleviate conflicts with parents from opposing teams, it will also send a clear message to our children that their opponent should be respected as a worthy opponent rather than someone to be hated or jeered.

Representing Your Child's Team

While you are not actually a member of your child's team, you do represent her team and the organization or school that supports it. Remember that when you wear the team colors or logos or cheer for that team, you are serving as a representative for everyone else to observe. As parents, we encourage our children to be positive ambassadors for their teams and all other entities that support them. They have the right to expect the same from us. Avoid doing anything that will bring disgrace or embarrassment to your child and her team when you are representing them.

When Others Are Embarrassed to Sit Next to You

The importance of modeling the lessons of sportsmanship and general respect for all people involved in a competition was discussed in detail earlier in this book. However, one telltale sign that you need to police your own behavior at athletic events is when your spouse, significant other, family members or friends are too embarrassed to sit next to you because of the way you act. As previously mentioned, it is imperative that you model good sportsmanship, respect and composure if they are lessons you want your child to learn from sport. There is no way you are modeling those lessons if those who care about you most will not sit next to you because of your actions. Ask those closest to you such as a spouse or friend whether or not your behavior crosses the line from being supportive to being adversarial and negative in any manner. Then make the appropriate changes if needed.

Policing Other Parents

Parental Code of Ethics

Many schools, clubs and organizations are adopting a parental code of ethics to help hold parents more accountable for their actions. Parental behavior has become so problematic that some teams around the country are making it mandatory for parents to attend an orientation session, and read and sign a code of ethics before their children can participate. Have you had to read and sign a parental code of ethics? If not, I would encourage you to ask why. Better yet, rather than depending on administrators to devise a parental code of ethics, I would encourage you to work with the booster club or parent organization that supports your child's team and devise one. An example of a parental code of ethics is included in the appendix of this book. You can also view many examples of parental codes of ethics on the Internet. You wouldn't have to reinvent the wheel, so to speak. Use the example from this book or go to the web and search under "parental code of ethics" and you will see numerous examples you can use as a model.

Having a parental code of ethics certainly does not guarantee that everyone is going to demonstrate appropriate behavior at all times. However, it can be a powerful vehicle for making parents more aware of behaviors that are acceptable and unacceptable during athletic competitions.

Confronting Other Parents

While it is important to be proactive in helping establish and support a general code of ethics for all parents of athletes in your organization or school, it is a different matter if you attempt to personally confront individuals or groups that are not following the code of ethics. I would encourage you to be very cautious regarding any personal confrontation during a competition. This can be difficult if these people are making derogatory comments about your child. However, keep in mind that nothing positive will come from you confronting another parent when he or she is emotional or upset. This would be an appropriate time to involve administrators if this person is being overtly disrespectful and belligerent. They are trained to handle such situations in a manner that will more likely diffuse the situation rather than exacerbate it.

While it isn't advisable to confront emotional parents, some individuals have been very creative in policing the behavior of others. Two examples were brought to my attention when I was speaking to groups of parents and we were discussing the concept of parents policing their own ranks. The first example was provided by the mother of a girl on a junior varsity basketball team. A parent of one of the girls on the team always stood at the top of the bleachers and yelled derogatory remarks at the officials, coaches and even players. He made the people around him very uncomfortable, but was oblivious to the effect that his actions were having on others and how he sounded. So, this sport mother decided to videotape him during the games without his knowledge. She sat where he was unaware of her and videotaped him for several games. She then mailed the tape to him anonymously. She included a note that encouraged him to view it and see for himself how he looked and sounded when he acted the way he did. She said that from that point on, the man completely changed. He no longer yelled and screamed negative remarks. He was much more subdued and didn't bring as much attention to himself. After a while he began yelling again, but the yelling was encouraging and positive.

The second creative example of parents policing other parents was shared by the mother of a boy who played on a club soccer team. Parents that attended the soccer games were given lollipops before the games started. All parents knew they were supposed to put a lollipop in their mouths if they were being negative in any way. Most parents had fun with the idea and made a more concerted effort to cheer in a positive manner. As simple as they might seem, both of these strategies proved to be very effective in their respective situations. With a little creativity, you and the other parents at your school or organization can devise strategies to help all of you create a positive atmosphere on the sidelines. And remember, if you receive a videotape in the mail with an anonymous note, or get an extra lollipop at your child's competitions, someone might be trying to send you a message!

Warning Signs: Do You Have a Life of Your Own Outside Your Child's Sport?

There really isn't a much simpler way to say this: Make sure your commitments to your child's team still leave you with time for yourself. It isn't uncommon for athletes as young as eight or nine to have multiple practices and competitions in a week. As a result, parents spend most or all of their free time shuttling children between practices and competitions, eating at fast food restaurants, and staying in cheap motels. The question becomes, "Do you have a life of your own outside your child's sport?" The following are a few signs that you might be over-involved.

You Attend Most or All Practices

I personally know the parents of two different high school athletes who rearrange their work schedules and other aspects of their lives so they can attend their child's practices. One indicates he "just wants to have a feel for what's happening with the team." The second says he needs to be there so he can give his son feedback on how he is practicing.

Most parents don't take such drastic measures to attend practice, but some feel they need to be at every training session in order to be supportive. It is important to note that you might be sending the wrong message about keeping sport in the proper perspective when you feel you have to attend *all* practices. Even when your child is first starting a sport and you have become comfortable with her coach, it is appropriate to drop her off, inform her you will run errands or do something for yourself, and that you will be back in plenty of time to pick her up when practice is finished. By taking this approach, you will let her know that her sport is "her thing" and that she can enjoy it on her own without you having to be there at all times. I am certainly not saying that you never stay and watch practice—just not all of them.

As your child moves into middle and high school, you should feel it is appropriate to drop in every now and then, as long as your son or daughter gives you the permission to do so—yes, I think we need to ask their permission if we want to attend practice. As he gets older, he will likely be embarrassed or at least uncomfortable if you are always in attendance. The key is to communicate with your child as he matures and listen to his desires in this matter.

Your Family Vacations Revolve Around the Athlete's Sport

Family vacations can be some of the most memorable times for children. Unfortunately, more and more parents are choosing to combine their family vacations with their child's sport. Once again you are likely to be sending the wrong message about the appropriate perspective regarding sport in your family's life if this is the case. It is important to take some time as a family that is completely away from any organized sport. Allow your family to have a break from the pressures and "the grind" of the sport. When challenged, one father said his family does take family vacations that do not involve his high school son's sport. However, when asked to elaborate on their vacations, it turns out that the family often drives a motor home and the father will stop every few hundred miles and have his son run wind sprints up and down the side of the road so that he can stay sharp and in shape. It would be interesting to ask that athlete if he truly enjoys those "family vacations."

In addition to promoting the wrong message about the sport and its significance compared to other aspects of family life, these vacations often cause unnecessary stress for the athlete. You might be more likely to get frustrated with your child if she doesn't play very well when the whole family has taken this vacation so she could participate in the sport. Your child may begin to worry about letting you and other family members down and even feel guilty because everyone is spending their vacation time at the soccer field rather than on the beach because of her.

Your Circle of Friends Is Limited to the Parents of Other Athletes

Take the time to examine your circle of friends and social acquaintances. If most or all are somehow related to the sport your child competes in, you probably don't have much of a life outside that sport. If this is the case, make an effort to move outside this circle and spend time with adults who have other interests and can encourage you to expand yours. You will certainly send the message that your son or daughter's sport isn't everything to you.

The Main Topic of Conversation at Mealtime Is Your Child's Sport

Does your child's sport dominate the conversation at mealtime in your household? Once again, if this is the case in your family, there is a good chance your child is receiving the wrong message about the importance of her sport compared to other aspects of life. This doesn't mean that you should never talk about the sport during a meal. However, you should ask the athlete in your family if it is okay to discuss the sport. She might not want to talk about it during this time. If she says it is okay to discuss the sport during mealtime, it certainly shouldn't be the only topic of conversation. Encourage and allow all members of the family to discuss their interests as well. This will provide a much more healthy balance for you and your child.

You Spend Time in Internet Chat Rooms That Discuss Your Child's Team

The chat room phenomenon is clearly out of control in the college ranks, and is occurring more often at the high school and even youth levels in some parts of the country. For the sake of convenience, parents of athletes on the same team often develop an e-mail tree to keep everyone up to date with what is happening with the team. Unfortunately, some parents take advantage of this very useful tool and use it as an open forum to discuss issues with their child's team. Some parents take it even further and establish chat rooms with the sole purpose of discussing their child's team. Often, parents question coaching decisions, individual athletes and other aspects of the team process. I have personally witnessed how these actions have had a very negative effect on teams. At a minimum, this seems to be a very questionable practice on the part of parents. Don't allow yourself to get caught up in this potentially destructive abuse of technology.

In general, keep in mind that your interest and support are usually very much appreciated by your child. However, it is very easy to allow your child's sport to overtake your life. Examine your situation and determine if there are areas in which you need to regain control. You will find a new perspective very refreshing and it will help you send the proper message about your child's sport in the whole scheme of family life.

Avoid Basing Your Self-Esteem and Ego on Your Child's Performance

I have a son named Graham. He happens to be pretty fast when he runs and often races other children in our neighborhood. Guess who feels pretty good when he wins those races? You got it—his dad. I can almost feel my chest swell up with pride as he races across the finish line in first place. As mentioned earlier, if we are honest with ourselves, we all live vicariously through our children at some level. We do feel good when they do something well. Whether it is singing a solo at the school talent show, making really good grades in school or when they perform exceptionally well as athletes, we are happy for them and often feel better about ourselves. In essence, they are a reflection of us, and when they look good, we look good. And whether we are willing to admit it or not, when they look bad, we feel that we look bad at some level as well.

Richard Ford, a former college basketball player and current youth coach, a stay-at-home dad and co-director of the National Point Guard Camp, captures the essence of this situation very well. He says that as parents we want to create a supportive, positive athletic environment for our kids, yet we are also looking for affirmation that they are excelling in a culture of competition. Athletics provides a yardstick for that assessment in a very public way that can be anxiety-provoking. If our kids get a bad report card, we can work through that failure in the privacy of our living room. If our kids miss a shot, throw the ball away or pick clovers while the opponent hits a ball past them, that failure is on public display and we feel some sense of shame in a culture that values success and winning so highly.

Another point to consider here is that the only time some adults really ever receive any significant attention is when their children do something very well. This causes a problem because it makes it very difficult for them to separate their ego and self-esteem from the accomplishments of their children. As a result, they are less tolerant of mistakes or poor performances because it affects how they feel about themselves. In return, this causes the child to feel more pressure to perform well.

Hollywood has very effectively captured the concept of a parent basing his self-esteem on his son's performance in the movie titled *Searching for Bobby Fischer*. It is a story about a chess prodigy and the actions of his father when it is discovered that the child has an exceptional talent. I would encourage you to watch that film sometime and determine if you see any of your own characteristics in the father.

The following are further signs your self-esteem and ego *could* be too closely aligned with your child's athletic performance:

Your Mood Depends on Your Child's Performance

Are you in a much better mood at work or around the house when your child performs well or wins as opposed to when she performs poorly or her team loses? If so, you are most likely too emotionally involved in her sport. It is one thing to be down or even emotionally drained after she competes. However, it is important for you to regain perspective in this situation as soon as possible. You have to begin to separate how you feel about life or yourself from her performance. Certainly, keeping your child's sport experience in perspective from the very beginning will help in this matter.

You Have Fallen Into the "We" Syndrome

This is one of those situations where there is a fine line between being supportive of your child and having your ego and self-esteem too closely aligned with his athletic performance. Do you make statements such as the following? "*We* played really well today." "*We* didn't get a good seeding in the tournament." "*We* have a lot of work to do to be able to play at that level"? As innocent as they seem, statements such as these are potential signs that you might be too emotionally involved in your child's sport. Statements such as, "*She* played really well," "*The kids* didn't get a good seeding in the tournament," or "*He* has a lot of work to do to be able to play at that level," might be more appropriate.

The important thing to remember is that *you* are not the

one competing. Your child is the competitor. You have had your opportunity to compete. Whether you were the star who received many accolades, the frustrated athlete who very seldom got a chance to play or one who never participated in sport, it is important to remember that this experience is about your child. Allow him to play without considering yourself part of the team.

Avoid Viewing Money and Time You Spend as Investments for Which You Expect a Return

It is costing more and more for athletes to participate in sports at all levels and across all sports. It is now commonplace for athletes in public schools to have to pay for the right to play. Funding for extracurricular activities is being cut from state budgets and local school districts cannot afford the costs of equipment and facilities for all of their athletic teams. Many children are involved in club programs where fees range from affordable Parks and Recreation programs to very costly elite traveling clubs. Many parents hire specialty coaches for one-on-one training with their child that can cost up to $150 an hour. There are some parents who spend up to $75,000 a year to send their children to academies where the focus is on developing skills in a particular sport.

The bottom line is that participation in sport often requires a significant investment of money and time from an athlete's parents. And if you view this money and time as investments for which you expect a return, you will most likely react differently towards coaches, officials and your child if things aren't going the way you feel they should be going. The return most parents are hoping for would come in the form of a college scholarship or even a lucrative professional contract. However, the reality is that very few athletes will ever participate in organized sport after high school. An overwhelming majority of our children aren't talented enough to participate after high school, much less to earn an athletic scholarship.

The NCAA (National Collegiate Athletic Association) has provided some very insightful information regarding the chances of an athlete participating at the collegiate level. They examined six different sports and estimated the probability of an athlete participating in that sport after high school. Those sports were men's and women's basketball, and men's ice hockey, football, soccer and baseball. The results indicate that approximately 2.9 percent of high school senior boys playing interscholastic basketball will go on to play men's basketball at an NCAA member-institution. Women's basketball is 3.1 percent, baseball is 5.6 percent, football is 5.8 percent, men's hockey is 12.9 percent, and men's soccer is 5.7 percent. These percentages do not indicate what percentage will earn scholarships; rather, they indicate an estimate of athletes who will merely *compete* at any level (i.e., NAIA, Division I, II, III). Some of those athletes will receive scholarships and others will receive no aid for their athletic abilities. As you can imagine, the percentages go down even further when they estimate the numbers of athletes who go on to compete at the professional level. These statistics can be viewed by going to **www.ncaa.org** and clicking on the "Athletes and Academics" link.

Another example of why you shouldn't view the money and time you spend on your child's sport as investments for which you expect a return was shared with me by a high school athletic director. He oversees a high school athletic program with thirty-two sports and several hundred student athletes. His school had two banquets at the end of the 2002-2003 school year. One was an athletic awards banquet and the other an academic awards banquet. During the athletic banquet, all student athletes who were receiving athletic scholarships were recognized. Of those several hundred participating in sports, six earned an athletic scholarship. The total amount of money granted to all six student-athletes was around $40,000 for the year. Most of the money was distributed among athletes as partial scholarships. Only one athlete was awarded a full scholarship. A week later, the academic banquet was held and all students receiving scholarship money for their academic success were recognized. The total amount of money granted to those students was more than $250,000. The clear message in this story is that your child will have a much better chance of earning an academic scholarship than she will an athletic scholarship. Unfortunately, some parents place an inordinate amount of pressure on their children academically as well, but that is a subject for another book!

I would encourage you to pause and examine the amount of time and money you are currently spending on your child's sport and determine whether or not you should continue at your current rate. If you decide that you want to continue at the current rate, you must be willing to do it with a giving heart and let the time and money go. It should be noted however, the returns you can and should expect from your investment are that your child is well coached and your child consistently demonstrates a positive attitude and admirable effort.

A Word of Encouragement If You Are Not Involved

I have emphasized that some parents care too much about their child's sport experience. However, there are also parents who are apathetic towards their child's sport experience or are unable to be involved for various reasons. Many children are raised in families that are different from the traditional family unit of thirty years ago. Many family units have both parents working full time outside the home or consist of single parents who have very little time after family duties. Even if you are in one of these situations, it is important for you to attempt to be involved at some level. Your child most likely puts a great deal of time and effort into her sport and would like to know that you are somewhat interested. A few signs that you might not be involved enough with your child and her sport include never going to any competitions, never asking about the sport and her experience, never taking her to and from practice or competition and being unwilling to provide any financial support.

Following are a few ideas to help you become more involved in your child's sport. One way to do this is to look at your child's competition schedule and make arrangements to attend a select few competitions. If you are unable to watch her in person, take the time to ask your child about her sport. When talking to her, remember to avoid asking whether or not her team won. Rather, ask if she enjoyed herself and whether or not she and her team played well. You could also volunteer to help with occasional booster club activities. Whatever you choose to do, your child will most certainly appreciate your effort.

Key Points to Remember

- *Positive behavior in the stands begins with you.*
- *Always demonstrate respect for all athletes and their parents at competition.*
- *Keep your child's sport in perspective by having a life of your own outside his or her sport experience.*
- *Separate your self-esteem and ego from your child's performance in sport.*
- *Avoid viewing the time and money you spend on your child's sport experiences as investments for which you expect a return.*

Coaches

photo by Phil Travis

"This would actually be a great profession if all I had to do was coach the kids and help them improve. Unfortunately, there are too many parents who make it difficult for coaches to coach and kids to play because of the way they behave, particularly during games."

—Middle School Basketball Coach

- *Is your child competing for a quality coach?*
- *Are you and your child's coach "on the same page" in terms of the environment in which your child competes?*
- *Do you always use good judgment when approaching your child's coach?*
- *Do you ever talk badly about your child's coach in front of your child?*
- *Are you a parent who coaches your child from the stands?*

Agree on the Type of Sport Experience Your Child Should Have

It is imperative from the beginning that you are "on the same page" with the school district, club or league's philosophy of your child's sport experience. Is this organization concerned primarily with the development of all participants or does winning take precedence over the child's development? Find out if there is anything written in terms of a league or organizational philosophy or mission statement.

Once you have established the overall philosophy of the league or club, it will be important for you to decide if this is where you want your child to participate in sport. As long as you honestly have sport in the proper perspective and your child is on a recreational or club team, you should certainly look for other places for your child to participate if the team's philosophy does not align with yours. It will only create frustration and discontent for you and your child if you stay.

While your flexibility is limited (as it should be) to move your child to a different situation once she begins participating on school teams, you should still determine the school's philosophy before your child begins to participate. At least you will know the overall environment in which she will be competing each day.

Know Your Child's Coach

Once you determine the organization's philosophy, you should determine the philosophy and mission of your child's coach. Without question, every coach your child comes in contact with for any extended period of time has an opportunity to make a significant impact on his life. Making sure your child has a coach who has his best interest in mind is a key consideration for you as a parent.

Whether your child is in a recreational league or on a school team, his coach should conduct a preseason meeting for parents. If that doesn't occur, you should contact the coach to schedule a meeting so that you can find out more about this person and his or her beliefs concerning sport. Whether it is a meeting of all parents or just you and the coach, you should take this opportunity to ask logistical and philosophical questions such as the following.

- *What are your expectations for this team and my child?*
- *Where will practices be held?*
- *How often and how long will the team practice?*
- *What is your policy for missing practice?*
- *What is your philosophy of coaching?*
- *Where does winning fit into your philosophy?*
- *What lessons will my child learn as a result of being coached by you?*
- *How will you ensure he learns those lessons?*
- *How will you handle discipline issues?*

Once the coach responds to these questions, you will have a better understanding of what he or she will focus on with your child. If you disagree with some of the responses that you were given, you should not confront the coach in front of others. Instead, schedule a meeting with the coach and strive to come to some type of agreement as to your child's experience while playing for this coach.

Characteristics of Effective Coaches

I would like to preface this section by saying that the majority of coaches at the youth and high school levels are excellent communicators, motivators, and teachers of skills and strategies in their respective sports. Unfortunately, many of these good coaches are leaving the coaching ranks. They provide several reasons for leaving such as low pay, high levels of stress, and burnout. I hear from a surprisingly high number of coaches that one contributing factor to their stress levels and burnout is their relationships with the parents of some of the athletes they coach.

It is critical to keep in mind that no coach is perfect, and it is also inevitable that you will disagree with your child's coach at some point regarding your child's sport experience. However, most coaches have their hearts in the right place and really want to do what is best for *every* athlete on their teams. With that in mind, try to avoid hastily judging your child's coach and using your influence in any way to get him fired or to stop coaching.

While you shouldn't demand perfection from coaches, there are several attributes you should be able to expect from anyone coaching your child. Volunteer coaches at the youth level should be able to demonstrate some level of proficiency in the following:

- *Develops a philosophy of coaching appropriate for the level he or she is coaching.*
- *Encourages athletes to have fun.*

- *Provides a positive environment.*
- *Knows the basic rules and strategies of the sport.*
- *Has the ability to teach the basic skills of the sport.*
- *Has the ability to adapt to various skill levels of the athletes.*
- *Models good sportsmanship.*
- *Demonstrates knowledge of basic first aid.*

As your child begins to compete at the middle school level or is playing for a coach who is paid for coaching, you should be able to expect more from that person. Administrators in authority over these coaches should ensure that they have participated in various training sessions that equip them to be quality coaches. In our extensive work with some of the most successful and credible coaches in the world, Jeff Janssen and I have established a model for success we feel coaches should strive for in their development. We highlight the characteristics of successful coaches in our book *The Seven Secrets of Successful Coaches: How to Unlock and Unleash Your Team's Full Potential.* These characteristics demonstrate a coach's credibility and his or her ability to lead people. Credible coaches are character-based, competent, committed, caring, confidence builders, communicators, and consistent. Hopefully your child's coaches are striving to exemplify these characteristics on a daily basis.

Coaches Who Are Character-Based

- Focus on being honorable people with high ethical standards who seek to "do the right thing."
- Tell the truth to their athletes and don't manipulate or play mind games.
- Take pride in representing their teams and athletes with dignity.

- Emphasize character development with their athletes because they know that character is just as important as skill in the long run.

Coaches Who Are Competent

- Possess a thorough understanding of the strategies and fundamentals of their sport.
- Realize the importance of being inquisitive despite having a solid understanding of Xs and Os.
- Continually look for new and innovative ways to coach.
- Are able to admit limitations and mistakes.
- Maintain a humble nature and are able to keep success in perspective.

Coaches Who Are Committed

- Create successful visions for their teams.
- Have a true passion for sport and coaching.
- Have incredible reserves of energy and resiliency.
- Enjoy competing without placing winning above all else.

Coaches Who Are Caring

- Care about their athletes as people.
- Sincerely want the best for their athletes.
- Invest the time to get to know each of their athletes on a personal level.
- Spend some time with injured and little used members of the team.
- Serve as an advocate for their athletes at school and in the community.
- Help their athletes long after their eligibility is finished.

Coaches Who Are Confidence-Builders

- Plant seeds of success in their athletes' minds and convince them that they can and will be successful.
- Have a special knack for making people feel good about themselves.
- Demand and set high standards, yet are patient enough to help athletes develop.
- Have the ability to motivate athletes without belittling or embarrassing them.

Coaches Who Are Great Communicators

- Strive to be open, honest and direct when communicating with individuals and the team.
- Continually remind and refocus people on what they need to do to be successful.
- Involve their athletes as much as possible and value the input they provide.
- Have the remarkable ability to truly listen to their athletes.
- Proactively address concerns and conflicts before they become major problems or distractions.

Coaches Who Are Consistent

- Develop a sound philosophy of coaching that remains stable over time, yet flexible enough to adapt to changing situations or times.
- Bring a productive and consistent mood to practices and games, regardless of whether their team is winning or losing.
- Avoid allowing the highs to get too high or the lows to get too low.

- Have few rules, but are consistent in how they apply them regardless of the different roles athletes play on a team.
- Take pride in the organization of their practice and game preparation.

As you evaluate your child's coach, remember these are characteristics that all coaches should *strive* for throughout their careers. It is very rare for a coach to exhibit all of these characteristics at all times. Don't be too quick to judge your child's coaches, and avoid using these suggested characteristics as ammunition against them. Rather, encourage them and support them as much as possible. If you do feel you need to talk to a coach at some point, there are appropriate ways to discuss various issues.

Approaching Your Child's Coach

This issue is by far the most frustrating aspect of the parent-coach relationship for most coaches, and it seems to be one of the aspects of sport that has changed most dramatically over the last twenty to thirty years. Parents today are much more likely to speak to the coach regarding a wide array of issues than they were in the past. I know that as an athlete, I would have cringed if either of my parents had spoken to any of my coaches on my behalf. Granted, there have been coaches that should have been confronted because of their abusive treatment of athletes. However, parents today are much more involved in their child's sport experience. This can be more of a problem than it is helpful. Following are a few reminders to help you use your best judgment regarding communication with a coach.

When You Observe Negative Behavior by the Coach

Parents typically confront a coach when their child complains about the coach or when they personally observe certain behaviors by a coach. Earlier in this chapter you were provided a brief synopsis of what to look for in a coach, and hopefully your child's coach is striving to consistently demonstrate those qualities at a high level. The following are a few examples of behaviors that would warrant you confronting your child's coach.

- Coach continually berates your child in front of others in order to embarrass or belittle him.
- Coach uses personal attacks when instructing athletes, rather than focusing on the athlete's behavior.
- It is clear that coach values winning over everything else.
- Coach is cheating in some manner or teaches athletes how to cheat.
- Coach is not being a good role model for athletes during and away from the sport.

When Your Child Complains About the Coach

The first thing you must remember if your child is complaining about a coach is that you are hearing only one side of the issue. It is also important to realize you might only see your child at competition time and the coach is with him for the other 95 percent of the time. Your child might be biased and it is important to be as objective as possible when you are listening in this situation. Ask your child to provide specific examples to support his issue with the coach. Listen as objectively as possible without defending either your child or the coach right away and then use your best judgment as to whether anyone should talk to the coach.

Once you feel you have all the pertinent information, you have a few options. You can provide your child strategies for making the most of the situation, or, depending on the age of your child, you can either speak to the coach or have him speak to the coach directly. Certainly, you can't expect a nine- or ten-year-old to confront a coach, but if your child is competing at the middle school level and above, you should encourage him to confront the coach first. It is a great life lesson for your child to learn when he must confront a person of authority. Too many times parents want to intervene right away for their child and don't take the opportunity to help their child develop this very important skill. This might be very difficult for him to do, but it will benefit him greatly in the long term. The coach will also have a greater respect for him than if you intervene first. If the issue still isn't settled once your child has talked to the coach, then you might consider contacting the coach to determine if you and your child can discuss the issue with him or her.

Strategies for Effectively Approaching a Coach

Once you have determined that you must talk to the coach regarding a certain issue, it is important to follow a few key guidelines to ensure you handle it appropriately.

Always Approach in a Positive Manner

The first thing you must remember about approaching a coach is that it shouldn't be viewed as a competitive confrontation where someone should be declared the winner when it is finished. It also shouldn't be viewed as an opportunity for you to "put the coach in her place." Rather, it should be viewed as an opportunity to get the coach to examine her behavior as objectively as possible without becoming defensive.

One very effective way to accomplish this is to use a positive approach to provide feedback. Essentially, you begin by pointing out aspects of coaching that the coach is doing well. For example, "You have a very creative mind when it comes to designing offenses" or, "My son really appreciates that you obviously care about him more than just as an athlete who can help you win." By doing this, the coach will be less likely to be defensive from the beginning.

The second phase involves you providing specific feedback regarding the area of your concern. This should be done in a manner where you aren't judging the coach. Rather, you should merely point out what is occurring and how it is affecting your child. For example, "You seem to regularly belittle and embarrass my daughter in front of others. She often comes home crying after practice" or, "My son told me the other day that you were teaching him how to cheat during games. I really want him to learn how to play the game honestly."

Once you have provided specific feedback, you should end the conversation on a positive note. For example, "I know you don't mean anything personally when you make negative comments to my daughter in front of others and I appreciate your willingness to listen to me today" or, "I appreciate your competitiveness and desire to win and I believe you are a good role model for my son. I believe you teach my son how to play the game the right way." Ending this way will help the coach focus more on the message that was being sent and make him much more likely to take into consideration what was being said.

Never in Front of Other People

Unless a child is in immediate danger, approaching a coach in front of other people will rarely result in a productive outcome. Keep in mind that you most likely wouldn't want anyone to approach you in front of others. By avoiding public confrontations where the exchange might become volatile, you will also be modeling restraint to your child.

Twenty-Four-Hour Rule

One very effective method to help you avoid approaching a coach in front of others is to allow yourself twenty-four hours to think about it. By adhering to this timeline, you will have an opportunity to think about what you want to say. You will likely be much less emotional about the situation. In fact, you might decide that you don't really need to say anything after having time to think about it.

Never Over E-mail

Some parents do not approach a coach in front of others, but they use other media to convey their frustrations. However, using e-mail to confront a coach is not appropriate. At first glance, it might appear that it would be an effective way to say what is on your mind because voice inflection and emotion aren't as evident in an e-mail. However, you can make some very hateful and sometimes regrettable remarks through a computer. E-mail is a great way to communicate with a coach regarding the logistics of practice, competitions and other daily activities with the sport. Just make sure it isn't used to vent your anger.

Never Call the Coach at Home

Another way parents approach a coach without doing it in front of others is to call her at home. This should never occur. Coaches need to be able to have time away from their sport. Some have families they want to spend time with when away from the sport. Others merely need to have that time to "refuel their tanks." It demonstrates a general lack of respect for your child's coach if you call her at home to confront her.

Once you are in a situation to constructively approach your child's coach, there are two areas that you should use particular caution with in conversations with him or her.

Playing Time

There are very few parents who are always happy with the playing time their children get during competition. Therefore, it is an area that most parents want to discuss with the coach. If you are a parent who attempts to discuss your child's playing time, you have to ask yourself why you want to confront him. If we are honest with ourselves, our own egos and the time and money we invest are very often the reasons we confront coaches over playing time. Is the reason you want to confront the coach because you are embarrassed when your child doesn't get to play as much as other children? Or is it because you have invested significant time and money in your child's sport and you feel you and your child are being cheated out of playing time? Neither of these is a proper reason to confront a coach. It is important to remember that most coaches are going to give their teams the best opportunity to be successful. Therefore, if the coach feels your child will help in this goal, your child will participate.

It is also important to remember that athletes have no control over their playing time. They do, however, have complete control over how hard they work and the type of attitude they display in practice. That is what should be emphasized with athletes rather than talking to their coach about playing time.

If after considering all of this you still feel you must talk to your child's coach about playing time, say that your child wants to play more and you want to know what she can do to improve her skills. Then be willing to help her improve those skills without taking your involvement to an extreme.

Other Athletes on the Team

This is a topic that should always be off limits in discussions with a coach. For example, asking questions such as, "Why is Johnny or Suzy starting in front of my child?" or, "Why does my child get the least amount of playing time on the team?" should be avoided. Once again, your child has no control over how others are doing or how much they are playing. Make sure your discussions with the coach revolve around what your child can do to improve. Talking about other children will only serve to cause friction between you and the coach.

Make the Coach Your Ally

I recently had an opportunity to spend a significant amount of time with a very talented high school basketball player and her family. As I began to listen to the parents, I noticed that they often spoke badly of their daughter's coach in front of her. I could see in her body language that it made her uncomfortable, and she confirmed this by saying, "I wish Mom and Dad didn't talk bad about Coach all of the time. He isn't perfect. I don't necessarily love playing for him, but he is my coach and I have to try to get along with him."

In situations such as this, the athlete is always caught in the middle. Athletes want to please their coaches because that person dictates their playing time and the roles they have on the team. They also seek approval from and want to please their parents (most of the time). Therefore, athletes are forced to take sides and either agree with the negative comments about the coach or attempt to defend him or her. In essence this creates a division of loyalties for the child.

I would encourage you to take a moment to reflect on whether you make derogatory comments about your child's coach in front of him. If so, it is important that you make an effort to avoid succumbing to the temptation to talk bad about the coach when your athlete is within earshot. If you must bad-mouth the coach, wait until your child has gone to bed or isn't around and then you can vent your frustrations to your significant other.

Leave the Coaching to the Coaches

Second-guessing the coach has most likely been a part of sport since the first organized games were played. It seems that everyone becomes an expert on the sidelines. It is one thing when this occurs in large stadiums where the chatter from those in the stands is drowned out by the overall noise. However, it is a different matter when parents are coaching their children from the sidelines. While you might think you are being helpful when you provide instructions to your child as she plays, you are in fact doing more harm than good in many situations.

It is impossible for your child to consciously pay attention to more than one thing at a time. For a relevant example, think about the last time you were at a party or in a crowd of people and you were involved in a conversation with someone. As you were listening to this person talk, you suddenly became aware of a more interesting conversation behind you. Your attention was then diverted to that conversation and you were no longer able to pay full attention to the person in front of you. Both conversations were competing for your attention and you were unable to give both your *undivided* attention. This is the same phenomenon your child experiences when she is attempting to play, listen to the coach and listen to you all at the same time. Your child cannot do all three at one time and you undermine her ability to concentrate when you coach her from the sidelines.

This phenomenon became such an issue for the Northern Ohio Girls' Soccer League that they devised a plan to provide their soccer players with an environment where they could play the game without being coached by their parents. In 1999, league officials designated one Sunday as "Silent Sunday." Parents in attendance at any games were only allowed to cheer for their children in a positive manner without providing any instructions. A few of the coaches in that league have indicated that their players probably wished every Sunday was Silent Sunday because they enjoyed the opportunity to play soccer without having to worry about listening to instructions from their parents. This league has adopted regular Silent Sundays and other leagues around the country have followed their lead.

As children get older, they become more adept at tuning their parents out and focusing more on the game itself, but until the point where you become background noise for your child, allow the coach to coach and spend your time and energy cheering for your child.

Key Points to Remember

- *Ensure your child is playing for a quality coach.*
- *Make sure you and your child's coach are "on the same page" regarding what your child's sport experience should be like.*
- *Use effective communication techniques when you feel you must confront your child's coach.*
- *Make sure you and your child's coach work together as allies, rather than against each other, to ensure your child has a successful sport experience.*
- *Allow your child to compete without you coaching him or her from the sidelines.*

Your Athlete In and Around Competition

photo: New Jersey High School Athletic Association

"I would give all of my individual awards and accomplishments back if I just knew my dad loved me unconditionally. The pressure I felt from him to play well and win every time I was on the field was incredible."

—Former College All-American and Olympic Athlete

- How do you respond when your child makes a mistake during competition?
- Are you overly emotional when your child loses a competition or doesn't play well?
- Do you treat your child differently when she wins as opposed to when she loses a competition?
- Are you the coach of your child's team? If so, do you treat your child in a manner consistent with other athletes on the team?
- Do you build, rather than destroy, your child's confidence in the way that you interact with him?

Build, Rather Than Destroy, Confidence

In an ideal world, children wouldn't depend too heavily on their parents and coaches to help build their confidence. They would rely on their own beliefs about their abilities to be successful. The reality is that a parent's confidence in a child will often become that child's confidence. Therefore, it is imperative that your words and actions build your child's confidence, rather than destroy it. Your goal should be to do your part to create an environment where your child is *pursuing success* instead of *avoiding failure*. The following are a few reminders that might help you in this area.

Avoid Showing Negative Emotions While Watching Your Child Perform

As mentioned in the previous chapter, there are many athletes who are keenly aware of the reactions of their parents, particularly when they fail. The main factor you must keep in mind if you react in a negative manner when your child fails is that you are very likely to create a fear of failure in him. What that means is that he will likely focus on avoiding failure or mistakes rather than focusing on performing well. It is important to realize that an athlete who is afraid of failing is much more timid, lacks assertiveness, is unwilling to take chances and thinks too much about her performance. Athletes often view negative reactions from parents as a sign of their failure, so a simple way for you to demonstrate confidence in your child is to allow her to play through mistakes during competition. You can do this by refraining from yelling your frustrations or showing your disappointment with poor body language. Instead, you should either say nothing or encourage her with positive verbal and nonverbal statements about her potential at the next opportunity.

To illustrate this point, the parents of a high school tennis player asked if I would spend some time with her to determine why she seemed to play tentatively in many of the matches she was supposed to win. It didn't take very long to determine that the girl was very aware of her father and his responses to her mistakes during matches. I observed the father during several matches and ended up spending much more time helping *him* learn how to respond to his daughter's mistakes or poor play than I spent with the athlete herself. Once he made an effort to be more encouraging, she relaxed and began playing much more consistently.

Most Mistakes Aren't Made on Purpose

I have never heard of an athlete at any level who purposely made a mistake during a competitive situation. Your child is likely doing everything she can to be successful while competing. One reason parents lose sight of this fact is that once again their egos get in the way. Parents often view their children as reflections of them and when the child makes a mistake, they think it makes them look bad. Be honest with yourself and determine if this is the case with you. If so, you must make a sincere effort to remove your ego from the situation and remember that your child really never makes a mistake on purpose.

Avoid Making It Personal

In an earlier section on talking to your athlete after competition, it was suggested to ask your child when it would be okay to discuss his performance. Once you provide your child with feedback, it is important to avoid attacking him as a person and focus on the behavior. Statements such as, "You were an embarrassment out there today," "You played horribly tonight," or, "Your younger brother can play better than you" are degrading personal statements about your child.

To assist you in having a more positive interaction with your child and focus more on the skill or behavior, you should use the positive approach to feedback as was discussed earlier (Approaching a Coach). Essentially, you begin by pointing out something your child did well. Imagine, for example, that you are the parent of a tennis player. You might begin with a statement such as, "You hustled today as much as I have ever seen you hustle." This will keep you from beginning the interaction in a negative manner and will decrease the likelihood of your child tuning you out from the beginning. The next phase of this feedback includes providing your child with specific, constructive feedback about the skill or aspect of her performance you are addressing. For example: "It seemed like you were taking your eyes off the ball as it crossed the net. Make sure you make it a priority to focus on the ball all the way into your racket the next time you practice." The final phase of the feedback includes a statement of reassurance or encouragement. For example: "I know you will get better if you continue to work as hard as you do." Using this approach will almost certainly result in a more constructive interaction between you and your child because she will not feel like she has to defend personal attacks by you.

Avoid Sarcasm, Belittlement and Embarrassment

No one really thrives on being embarrassed and belittled in front of other people. Some parents make the mistake of believing that if they do this to their child, the child will be less likely to make the same mistake or play poorly again. Once again, this often occurs because parents are living vicariously through their children, and when children don't perform well, the parent feels like it is a direct reflection on them.

Imagine how you might feel if your boss or superior was upset with your performance at work and began to belittle or embarrass you in front of your coworkers. It would most likely cause you to lose some measure of respect for that person. It might also affect your confidence in your own ability to be successful. Doing this to your child will only serve to undermine his confidence as well.

Utilize a 5-to-1 Ratio of Positive to Negative Statements

One strategy to help you avoid making it personal or using belittlement and embarrassment when trying to motivate your child is to make a conscious effort to verbalize many more posi-tive statements than negative statements. A ratio that has been found to be very effective in teaching and coaching is a ratio of 5-to-1. That means that for every statement from you that your child might perceive as being negative, you should give her five positive statements. These positive statements should be given with the same level of conviction and authenticity of negative statements you might provide. The last thing you want is for your child to perceive that your positive statements aren't genuine. Following this ratio will help you be a more positive sport parent and it will surely help your child feel more confident.

Provide a Healthy Perspective on Losing

I recently watched a middle school football game where both teams played very well. As expected, one team lost and I lingered to observe how the two teams would respond to the outcome. As I left the game, I happened to be walking behind the quarterback of the losing team. He played a tremendous game and was visibly upset. His mother and father and two siblings were walking with him to the bus. What I found interesting was that both parents and one of the siblings were also crying. As I listened, it was apparent that they were crying because their son and brother had lost the game.

The message you send if you cry when your child loses is that winning is paramount to your happiness. You absolutely should empathize with your child if he is upset over a loss. However, you should try to avoid getting caught up in the emotion of the outcome of a competition. Your child is the one who has competed and worked hard to be successful, and should not have to be concerned about whether or not your happiness depends on his athletic success.

Another example of parents not providing a healthy perspective is when they stop attending competitions because their child's team loses often. One father of a middle school football player in Kansas refused to continue to attend his son's games because in the father's mind the team wasn't very good and he couldn't handle watching them lose. This clearly sends the message that this father is only happy or willing to come support his son as long as his team is winning. This is unfair to this boy and places him in a very difficult position.

Provide Unconditional Love Regardless of the Outcome

A friend of mine, quoted at the beginning of this chapter, who happens to be a very successful college coach once talked to me about the relationship she had with her father as she was growing up participating in athletics. This coach was very successful as an athlete during her career, and was two-time NCAA player of the year. Her team won two NCAA championships and she was an Olympian in her sport. However, she told me she would give all of that back if she just knew that her father loved her unconditionally. She went on to tell how her father would treat her much differently when her team won than when they lost. It got to a point that he would not only not speak to her for a day or so when her team lost, he also wouldn't speak to his wife. This put enormous pressure on my friend because she was participating in a team sport and she had very little control over how well the other members of her team played. She dearly wanted to please her father and make him and her mother happy. She indicated that his conditional love and support drove her to succeed at a high level. Unfortunately, it was at the expense of a loving relationship with her father. She still resents him for the way he treated her during those formative years of her life and they rarely speak today.

Most parents aren't this drastic in their conditional love and support. It is often done in much more subtle ways. Some parents will not be quite as enthusiastic with their child after a loss. Some might give their child the cold shoulder after a loss. It is important for you to be aware of how you treat your child after a competition and make every effort to consistently support him.

If you have a very young child, you should always keep the mood light after a competition. You can hug her or give her a high five. Ask if she had fun and then ask what type of drink or snack she would like. She will very quickly forget about the competition and focus on the drink or snack. And that is a good habit for her to develop early on, as it will help her to more effectively deal with frustrating performances and defeats as she matures.

As your child gets older and takes losses harder, he will most likely want you to avoid patronizing him and telling him it will be okay. I would encourage you to talk to your child and find out what he wants from you after a tough loss or poor performance. You can do this with a child as young as nine or ten years old. He will tell you what he wants and it will be important for you to honor his wish.

Avoid Forcing Your Child to Talk to You Immediately After a Poor Performance

There is little doubt that one of the last things most children want to do after a poor performance is explain why they played the way they did or why they made the decisions they did while competing. I have always thought it would be interesting to be a fly on the wall in some of the van rides home from competitions where parents are giving their children the third degree regarding their performances.

It is one thing to force your child to talk to you immediately after a poor performance if she demonstrated poor sportsmanship or bad behavior in some way. However, if you are a parent who talks to your child about her performance immediately afterwards, you should seriously consider asking her if that is helpful. You can phrase it in a different way by asking her what she needs from you as her parent after a poor performance or a tough loss. To reinforce an earlier point, children as young as nine or ten will be able to articulate what they want from you as their parent in these types of situations.

You must remember, she is often frustrated and might need time to herself to process what happened. Ask her when she feels it would be appropriate to talk about it. Be prepared for her to say that she doesn't want to talk to you about it right away. If that is the case, it will be important for you to honor her wish. Most likely, she will eventually want to talk to you about it and get your advice. Give her the space and time she needs and she will appreciate you and your role as a supportive parent so much more.

Another very effective way to give your child the space she needs is to allow and even encourage her to ride with the team when returning from away competitions. Obviously, that isn't always possible, especially if your child competes on a club team. However, many parents will discourage their children from returning with the team as a matter of convenience for the parents. It is much easier to take the child directly home without having to go to the school or other central meeting place. One important factor you should keep in mind when contemplating this situation is that some of the most memorable times your child will have in sport will be on the bus or van rides home with her teammates. They will collectively celebrate great performances and victories as well as share in the difficulties following poor performances and tough defeats. Allow and encourage her to have those experiences if she so chooses.

Coaching Your Own Child

One of the most incredible experiences a parent can have is to coach your own child. If handled correctly, coaching your own child provides you the opportunity to share experiences with him that are rarely found in any other arena in life. The two of you can share in his development as an athlete and share in the joy of performing well in addition to the frustrations that go along with poor performances. As his coach, you also have a larger impact on whether or not he will have an overall positive experience and whether he learns the great life lessons sport can teach. In my experience, most parents who coach their own kids have their hearts in the right place and want to provide a good experience for their children. The following are a few ideas to help you ensure your child enjoys having you as his coach.

Make Sure Your Child Wants You to Be the Coach

The very first thing you should do when considering whether or not to coach your child is to ask him if it is okay with him if you coach. Most young children would be thrilled to have one of their parents coach their teams. However, as children get older, some feel this relationship places them in a difficult situation. Whatever the age of your child, take the time to ask if he would enjoy having you as his coach. Then be willing to step back and merely be a supportive parent if he says he would rather someone else coach him. Obviously it is a different story if coaching is your profession where your child attends school. In that case, you obviously shouldn't be expected to step back and just be a supportive parent, but you will have to work very hard to make sure that being your child's coach doesn't come between the relationship the two of you have as parent and child.

Be Consistent

When coaching your own child, the tendency is to either have much higher standards for your child or be more lenient on him than other athletes on the team. Most athletes would likely say their parent was much harder on them than other athletes on the team. On the surface, this practice seems to be an effective method of helping your child maximize her potential. However, if you aren't careful, it could cause a strain in your relationship with her.

Some of the most talented and successful athletes I have had the opportunity to spend time with say that the parent who coached them had a significant role in their development and success. What is interesting, though, is that several of these athletes had a less-than ideal relationship with that parent after that experience was over. For example, a quarterback in the NFL describes how his father was his high school football coach. His father was much tougher on him than anyone else and would often make him throw several hundred passes in the backyard on the night of a poor performance in a game. Often those Friday nights were cold, wet and lonely. He would also make his son watch film with him at home when all of his other teammates were enjoying their normal lives. The son's perception was also that his father was quicker to embarrass and belittle him in front of his teammates than he would other athletes. This athlete still harbors resentment towards his father to this day for some of the tactics he used.

There are a few parents who coach their children so they can provide them with more opportunities to play or start than they would have if someone else were coaching them. While this might give your child an advantage in terms of his playing time, it puts him at a distinct disadvantage with his teammates. Keep in mind that children and their parents know if a coach is deliberately playing favorites with the athletes on his or her team. Your child will likely be resented and your credibility will be lost among those you are trying to lead if it is perceived that you are playing favorites.

Clearly there is a balance here. You have to make every effort to treat your child as if he were any other athlete on your team. Avoid being more harsh or critical of him just as you avoid showing favoritism. Either of those scenarios put your child in a difficult situation and can affect his overall experience in the sport.

Separate Your Roles as Parent and Coach

One of the best strategies for helping you treat your child in a consistent manner along with all the other athletes is to distinguish between your role as the coach and your role as the parent. This might be very difficult for you to accomplish, but it is important to make a conscious effort to separate the two. One high school volleyball player put it in perspective for her mother who coached her and made no real effort to distinguish between her role as parent and coach. This coach was much more critical of her daughter during practice and competitions than she was of other athletes on the team and she would regularly continue to coach her daughter for several hours and sometimes days regarding a particular match. It got to a point where the athlete felt like she had no break from volleyball and she began to dread going to practice. One day after practice and a particularly difficult ride home, the athlete got to the front door, began to open it and suddenly slammed it shut. She then asked her mom, "When are you going to stop being my coach and start being my mom? You don't ever give me a break here and I'm going to quit if you don't start being my mom sometimes." The coach indicated this episode hit her like a ton of bricks. She had no idea she was losing perspective and causing so much anguish for her daughter. The coach and her daughter now have a much better relationship because the mother makes a conscious effort to separate the two roles she plays in her daughter's life. They have agreed to talk about volleyball on the ride home from practice or a match. Then once they step inside the house, there is no more discussion about volleyball. They both focus on other aspects of their lives. And both indicate they are enjoying their relationship much more now.

Always try to think about what is best for your child in the decisions you make and the actions you take. Continually monitor yourself and be willing to make needed adjustments in order to help your child enjoy her experience. Pushing your athlete to excel or giving her great opportunities to participate can be very positive. But it should never be at the expense of the personal relationship you and your child have with each other. That relationship is what you will have when your child's athletic career is finished.

Key Points to Remember

- *Allow your child to make mistakes in competition without having to worry about your response to those mistakes.*
- *Always provide unconditional love and support regardless of how your child performs.*
- *Always give your child the space he or she might need after a poor performance or tough loss.*
- *When you coach your own child, make sure you treat him or her as you would other athletes on the team.*
- *Never belittle or embarrass your child in front of others.*

Conclusion

photo by Phil Travis

I am often asked, "Don't you think kids are different today?"
My response is always that kids really haven't changed much,
but parents have changed. Kids still want to play sport because
of the many intrinsic values it offers. They still want someone to instill
discipline and teach them the sport. However, some parents are rob-
bing them of this experience because of their overinvolvement in their
sport experiences, their overemphasis on winning, and the pressures
that go along with that mind-set. Whether you are the parent of a
child just beginning to participate in sport or a seasoned veteran, you
have a tremendous opportunity to ensure your child will have a wonderful experience in sport.

In conclusion, I hope I have made you feel good about your behaviors as a sport parent. I also hope I have provided you with helpful strategies for any behaviors you might need to change. Keep the following in mind and you will go a long way towards doing your part as a successful sport parent.

- *Remember: They are kids and not adults. Do not be tempted to convey the professional and collegiate model of sports on youth and high school sports.*
- *Keep your ego under control. It isn't about you. It is about your child and his experience. Make sure every action you take and every decision you make are in the best interest of your child and not to boost your own ego or make you feel good. You have had your chance in sport and it is now your responsibility to make sure your child has a wonderful sport experience.*
- *Work with coaches and not against them. Remember that when you talk negatively about the coach in front of your child, you are creating a division of loyalty for her. This is never a good situation for her and she will constantly struggle with where her loyalties lie.*
- *Model the lessons you want your child to learn. As a sport parent, you can be a positive role model for these lessons by the way you act and react to various situations in sport. You must always remember your child is watching you and learning from everything you do. You never know when something you say or a reaction you have will make a lasting impact. Take pride in making sure not only that you talk about the great life lessons to be learned in sport, but also that you practice what you preach.*
- *Maintain a proper perspective. The main goals of sport at the youth and even the high school level should be to have fun, develop life skills and honor the game. Winning is important and is a part of sport and life. However, it should never take precedence over these other goals and should never be the sole measure of success.*
- *Remember that the overwhelming majority of athletes will be finished with their competitive athletic careers when they leave high school. Make sure you allow your child to enjoy that athletic journey.*

- *Evaluate yourself on a regular basis. Be self-reflective and ask yourself what it would be like to be your son or daughter and have you as a sport parent. Would that experience be a positive one? If your child is old enough, ask for feedback regarding how well you are playing the role of an effective sport parent. Then be willing to incorporate that feedback into your daily actions.*
- **Finally, as parents, we simply need to give the game back to the kids.**

Best of luck in this very rewarding, challenging, and important role that you have in your child's life. Play that role well and your child will very likely have a successful sport experience.

Appendix A:
Parental Code of Ethics

Parental Code of Ethics

The purpose of this Code of Ethics is to help you make a commitment to yourself, your child and everyone else you come in contact with during your child's athletic experience. Take the time to read each of these statements and truly make a commitment to adhering to them to the best of your ability.

I will always keep in mind that it is a privilege, rather than a right, for my child to participate in a sport.

I will always model good sportsmanship at competitions by the way I treat all athletes, coaches, officials and other fans.

I will insist that my child always demonstrate good sportsmanship and treat other athletes, coaches and officials with respect.

I will always teach my child how to win and lose with grace by the way I act in each of those situations.

I will always teach my child the importance of competing with integrity and will not help him or her cheat in any manner.

I will always remember that while I am not an athlete, I am representing my child's team at competitions.

I will always strive to work with my child's coach and not against him or her.

If I have an issue with a coach, I will always approach him or her in an appropriate manner.

I will always refrain from coaching my child immediately before, during and immediately after competitions because of the potential negative effect it may have on my child's performance.

I will always remember that I have had my opportunity in athletics and this experience is about my child.

I will have a basic understanding of the rules of my child's sport.

I will serve as a volunteer with my child's team or school as much as possible.

Parental Agreement
I have read each of these statements and I understand that if I make a commitment to abide by them, my child will have a much more enjoyable and successful sport experience.

Parent's Signature_____Date _____

References

Gough, R. (1997). *Character Is Everything: Promoting Ethical Excellence in Sport.* Fort Worth, Texas: Harcourt Brace and Co.

Hardy, C. & Crace, K. (1990). "Dealing with Injury." *Sport Psychology Training Bulletin,* 1 (6), 1-8.

Janssen, J. (2002). *Championship Teambuilding: What Every Coach Needs to Know to Build a Motivated, Committed and Cohesive Team,* Winning the Mental Game: Cary, NC.

Janssen, J. & Dale, G. (2001). *The Seven Secrets of Successful Coaches: How to Unlock and Unleash Your Team's Full Potential.* Cary, NC: Winning the Mental Game.

Pennington, B. (February 22, 2005). "Doctors See a Big Rise in Injuries for Young Athletes." New York *Times.*

Petipas, A. & Danish, S. (1995). "Caring for Injured Athletes." In S. Murphy (Ed.) *Sport Psychology Interventions* (pp. 255-281). Champaign, IL: Human Kinetics.

Searching for Bobby Fischer (May 29, 2001, Paramount Studios), based on the book by Fred Waitzkin and directed by Steve Zaillian.

About Greg Dale

Dr. Greg Dale is an Associate Professor and Mental Training Coach at Duke University. As a professor, Greg teaches and conducts research in the areas of Sport Psychology and Sport Ethics. As a mental training coach, Greg helps coaches and athletes develop systematic approaches to the mental aspects of performance. In addition to his work with athletes and coaches at Duke, Greg consults with coaches and athletes in professional football, soccer, baseball, golf, track and field, and tennis.

Greg was a middle and high school coach in New York City and San Antonio, Texas. He has conducted over two hundred workshops with coaches and athletes from a variety of high schools and colleges across the country and Mexico. He is a certified sport psychology consultant by the Association for the Advancement of Applied Sport Psychology and is a member of the sport psychology staff for USA Track and Field.

In addition to this book, Greg has coauthored the books *The*

Seven Secrets of Successful Coaches: How to Unlock and Unleash Your Team's Full Potential and *101 Teambuilding Activities: Ideas Every Coach Can Use to Enhance Teamwork, Communication and Trust.* He also has written and hosted a series of eleven videos for coaches and athletes.

Workshops by Greg Dale

Developing the Credible Coach: A Model for Success

This workshop is based on Dr. Dale's book, *The Seven Secrets of Successful Coaches: How to Unlock and Unleash Your Team's Full Potential* and is geared towards coaches. It emphasizes the importance of earning credibility with athletes as well as the dynamics of group development and productivity. Numerous recommendations are made to build effective leadership skills while also building high-performing teams.

Maximizing Your Potential: A Model for Performance Excellence

This workshop challenges athletes to extend their comfort zones and critically examine their approach to excellence. Topics covered in this workshop include preparing for success, embracing the pressure, trusting your instincts, effective goal-setting, perseverance in difficult situations and leadership skills. Application of these skills to areas outside of athletics is reinforced throughout the presentation.

Teambuilding 101: Keys to Enhancing Teamwork, Communication and Trust

This interactive workshop is based on Dr. Dale's book *101 Teambuilding Activities: Ideas Every Coach Can Use to Enhance Teamwork, Communication and Trust*. As a result of participating in this workshop, athletes on a team will have a better understanding of the need to work as a cohesive unit to accomplish team goals. Coaches who participate will gain in-depth knowledge of the teambuilding process. Specifically, both groups will have an opportunity to experience several activities that promote teamwork, communication, trust and positive team culture.

The Sport Parent: Helping Your Child Maximize His or Her Potential

Parents play a crucial role in determining whether or not children have a positive experience in sport. This thought-provoking workshop encourages parents to analyze the type of environment they are creating for their children. Topics covered in this workshop include the significance of the coach-athlete-parent triangle, lessons parents want children to learn from sport and the importance of modeling those lessons and effective goal-setting that parents can use with their children.

Coach, Athlete and Parent Products

Books

The Seven Secrets of Successful Coaches: How to Unlock and Unleash Your Team's Full Potential—$29.95
101 Teambuilding Activities: Ideas Every Coach Can Use to Enhance Teamwork, Communication and Trust—$24.95

Videos for Coaches
The Coach's Guide to Teambuilding—$39.95 (VHS and DVD)
Goal-Setting for Success: A Coach's Guide—$39.95 (VHS and DVD)
Coaching the Perfectionist Athlete—$39.95 (DVD)
Building the Athlete's Confidence: A Coach's Guide—$39.95 (DVD)
The Coach, Athlete and Parent Triangle: The Coach's Guide—$39.95 (DVD)

Videos for Athletes
Becoming a Champion Athlete: Making Every Practice Count—$29.95 (VHS and DVD)
Becoming a Champion Athlete: Mastering Pressure Situations—$29.95 (VHS and DVD)
Becoming a Champion Athlete: Goal-Setting for Success—$29.95 (VHS and DVD)
Becoming a Champion Athlete: Regaining Lost Confidence—$29.95 (DVD)

Videos for Parents
The Coach, Athlete and Parent Triangle: The Parent's Guide— $29.95 (DVD)
Visit www.excellenceinperformance.com or call 919-401-9640.

The Fulfilling Ride

A Parent's Guide to Helping Athletes Have a Successful Sport Experience

Greg Dale, Ph.D.

To order additional copies of this book
Call: **919-401-9640**
Visit: **www.excellenceinperformance.com**
Or mail check, money order, or credit card information to:

Excellence in Performance
11 Chimney Top Ct.
Durham, NC 27705

Name _____

School _____

Sport _____

Address _____

City, State, Zip _____

Country _____

Phone _____

E-mail_____

Credit Card _____

Exp. _____